Hit It!
History of
Tools

Dona Herweck Rice

Consultant

Timothy Rasinski, Ph.D.
Kent State University

Publishing Credits

Dona Herweck Rice, *Editor-in-Chief*

Robin Erickson, *Production Director*

Lee Aucoin, *Creative Director*

Conni Medina, M.A.Ed., *Editorial Director*

Jamey Acosta, *Editor*

Heidi Kellenberger, *Editor*

Lexa Hoang, *Designer*

Lesley Palmer, *Designer*

Stephanie Reid, *Photo Editor*

Rachelle Cracchiolo, M.S.Ed., *Publisher*

Based on writing from *TIME For Kids*.

TIME For Kids and the *TIME For Kids* logo are registered trademarks of TIME Inc. Used under license.

Teacher Created Materials

5301 Oceanus Drive
Huntington Beach, CA 92649-1030
http://www.tcmpub.com

ISBN 978-1-4333-3680-5

© 2012 Teacher Created Materials, Inc.
Printed in China
Nordica.072018.CA21800640

Table of Contents

Dig In! 4

The Nuts and Bolts 6

Nailing It 14

Tools of the Trade 20

Thc Finishing Touch. 28

Glossary. 30

Index 31

About the Author 32

Dig In!

She picks up the sticks. She looks at them closely and thinks about what to do. She points the sticks down and works to grab her food. It is hard to do, but she keeps trying. Then, finally, success! She puts the food to her mouth and eats.

But the sticks are not chopsticks, and she is not human. She is a chimpanzee. She uses the sticks to scoop up termites for her dinner. The tools make her life a little easier.

Throughout time, people have made tools to do many different things, including to eat. But it is amazing to think that other animals use tools, too!

A chimpanzee eats termites using a long stick.

Chopsticks (筷子)

Chopsticks are used like **tongs** to pick up food or to push it into a person's mouth straight from a bowl. They were first used in China around 5,000 years ago. Along with knives, they are among the earliest man-made eating **utensils** we know.

The Nuts and Bolts

What is the point of making and using tools? Tools get the job done, whatever it is.

The brain is amazing. There is not much the brain can imagine that it cannot figure out how to make happen—no matter how impossible it seems at first. For example, long ago in ancient Egypt, people built enormous pyramids that still stand. How did they do it? After all, they did not have the modern cranes, bulldozers, and other powerful **equipment** we have now. But they used their brains to figure out the right tools, **materials**, and equipment. We see the results of their work today rising from the desert sand.

Ancient Egyptians used tools to create the towering pyramids we see today.

Tool or Equipment?

What's the difference? Equipment is something used for a specific purpose. For example, a helmet is a piece of equipment used to protect the head. Tools are things that are made or used to do work. A hammer is a tool that is made to pound nails.

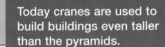

Today cranes are used to build buildings even taller than the pyramids.

Have people always used tools? Yes, they have, in one way or another. At first, tools were simply found objects that were used to do certain jobs. Think of the stick used by the chimpanzee to get food. People have always used these kinds of tools.

From around 10,000 B.C. to 2,500 B.C., people made tools from stones. This period is called the **Stone Age.**

In fact, people still use the things they find as tools. Have you ever camped and needed to pitch a tent? It is too hard to drive the stakes into the ground with your bare hands. Sometimes, people do not think to bring along a hammer when they camp. So, what can you use to pound a stake when a hammer is not available? How about a rock? Rocks were some of the very first tools, and they still come in handy!

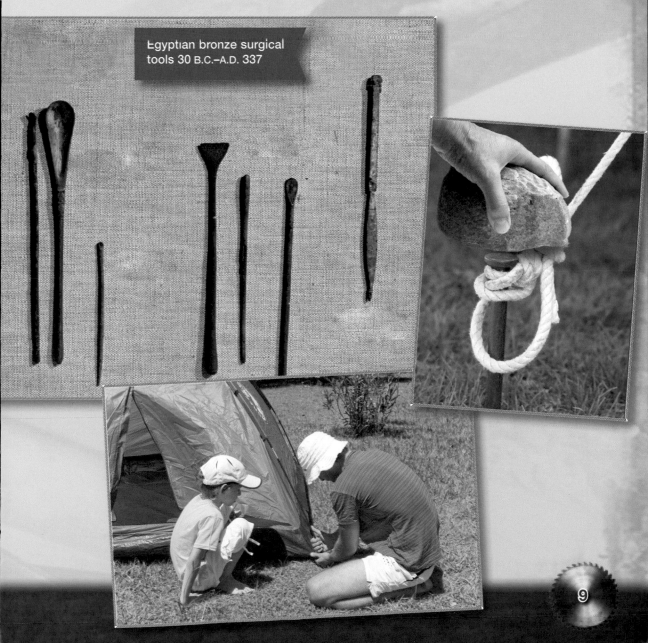

Egyptian bronze surgical tools 30 B.C.–A.D. 337

Can you guess the first tool ever used by people? It is something we are born with: hands. Think of the ways you use your hands as tools every day. Have an itch? Hands are an amazing itch-scratching tool. Drop something? Hands can work like a claw to grab it. You can use your hands to play the drums, flick light switches, or use video-game controllers. The list goes on and on. How many other tools do you know that can do so many things?

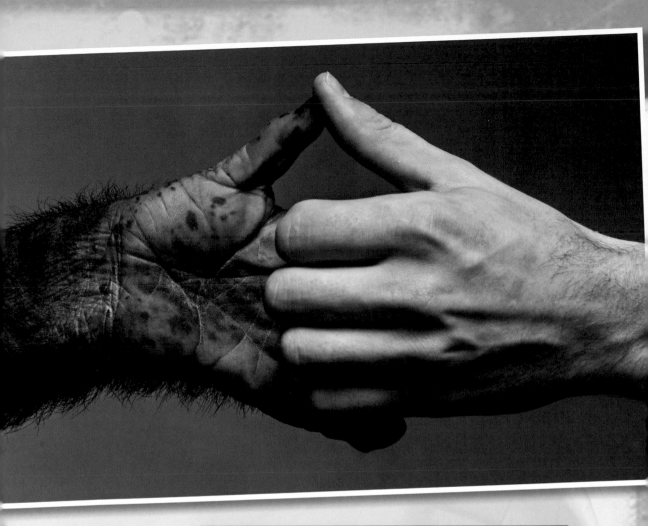

Opposable Thumbs

What makes human hands so amazing?
Opposable thumbs. These are thumbs that
can move opposite to the fingers on the same
hand. They allow humans to grasp and grip
objects. A few other species in the animal
kingdom also have opposable thumbs.

Over time, people realized they could make tools for specific purposes. When they saw a need for a tool, they could make a tool to fill that need. Sticks, stones, shells, antlers, and other items they found could be turned into more advanced tools. A sharpened stone could be attached to the end of a stick to make an arrow. A flexible piece of wood and a strand of **sinew** could be made into a bow. Many early tools were made from these types of simple supplies and a little creative thinking.

This woman uses a bow and arrow like those from around the 11th century A.D.

Around the world, people have made arrowheads like these by sharpening a hard stone to a point.

Tools for Animals

Many animals use objects they find as tools. Here are just a few examples. Elephants move large objects to stand on to get food that is out of reach. Sea otters use stones to knock shells off rocks. Parrots use old feathers to scratch the backs of their necks. And gorillas use sticks to help them walk upright when they cross high water.

This monkey uses a rock to break open a piece of food.

Nailing It

Advances in people's lives came quickly once they figured out how to make tools. They were able to do more things and do them better and more easily than before. Even hunting for food became easier. This gave people time to focus on improving their lives in other ways.

Horse-drawn plows like this one helped farmers turn the land.

hatchet

A water mill is a machine that uses water pressure to make energy.

A windmill creates and stores energy when the wind rotates the mill's sails.

People made tools to do things their bodies could not do. They could not kill prey with their hands and teeth. So they made bows and arrows, spears, and **hatchets**. When people learned how to use metal to make tools, they were able to become better farmers. They developed new power sources when they learned to make windmills and water mills. The mills captured the energy of the wind and the water.

Craftspeople throughout the **Middle Ages** and beyond came to depend on tools to earn a living. In earlier days, tools had to be made by hand. That takes time and a lot of skill. If a tool was lost or broken, a person couldn't simply run to the **hardware store**. The old tool would have to be fixed, or a new one would have to be made.

The Middle Ages lasted from about the 5th century to the 15th century.

woodworkers from the 15th century

woodworking chisels

Over time, a wide variety of metal tools such as these were developed.

By 1800, the cost of a craftsperson's chest of tools was equal to about one whole year's pay. Tools were precious. They were passed down from parents to children. Each owner marked the tools with his or her name so that no one else could claim them.

During the **Industrial Revolution**, people learned new ways to use tools to make other tools. People are the only animals that do this. Whole factories were built to make tools. These tools were used to make things people needed and wanted. At first, people ran the machines. Today many machines are run by other machines.

Women began working in factories more often during World War II.

Early blacksmiths often used tools like clamps and hammers to make more useful tools.

New Tools

Some people believe we are now in another revolution. Computers allow us to create new machines. We are learning to make tools that can only be seen through microscopes. We are working with **molecules** and **atoms** to do things people could not imagine even a few years ago. The tools we use are changing all the time. But the need for tools never changes!

Tools of the Trade

Tools are used in many **trades**. A chef uses kitchen tools. A tailor uses sewing tools. But the tools most people think of are the tools used to build things. These tools date back through history. In some instances, they have not changed much. When a good tool is well designed, there is not much that can be done to improve it. The following pages give some of the history of these interesting tools.

Every trade has its tools.

sewing tools

There has not always been forward progress in the development of tools. Some ancient Roman craftspeople had more advanced tools than similar craftspeople of the Middle Ages.

The ancient Romans built a complex water system, using advanced tools.

kitchen tools

Axes and Saws

The first axes were made as early as 8000 B.C. They were made from animal antlers. Axes were made from metal 5,000 years later. Axes like the ones we use today appeared about 500 B.C.

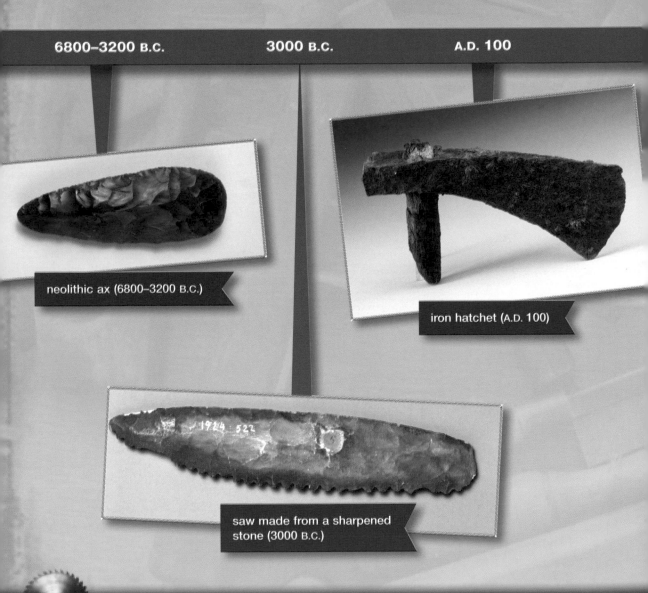

6800–3200 B.C. 3000 B.C. A.D. 100

neolithic ax (6800–3200 B.C.)

iron hatchet (A.D. 100)

saw made from a sharpened stone (3000 B.C.)

Ancient Egyptians made copper saws. Ancient Greeks and Romans added wooden handles. In the late 1600s and later, steel saws were created. Many different kinds of saws were made in order to do all types of work. These saws were important for furniture makers. They needed special saws to get different results.

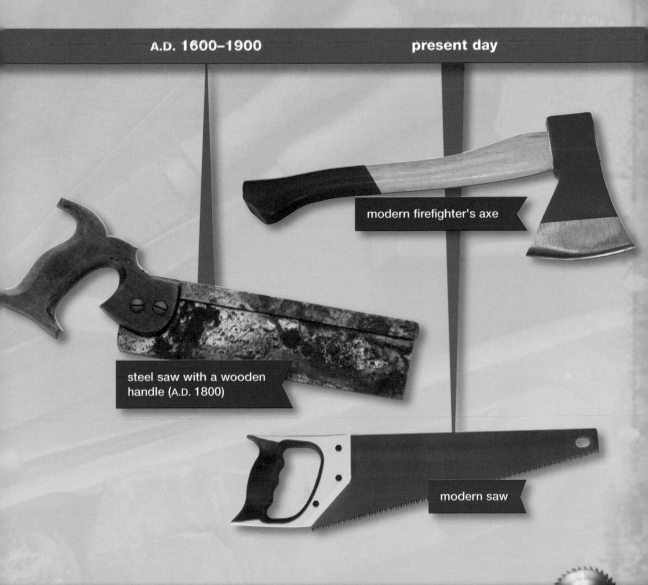

A.D. 1600–1900

present day

modern firefighter's axe

steel saw with a wooden handle (A.D. 1800)

modern saw

ancient hammer

modern hammer

Hammers and Pliers

The first hammers were just stones held in the hand. Ancient Greeks added handles. Ancient Romans added claws for pulling out nails. Different trades have made different hammers to do the kinds of work that needs to be done. But the basic hammer has stayed much the same.

Pliers are used to hold, grip, bend, and cut objects. Tongs, which are like early pliers, were first used to handle hot objects such as coals. Ancient Romans used iron tongs to hold hot metal. Today we use pliers to grip small objects and bend or cut wire. Modern pliers were not made until the 1700s.

blacksmith tongs

stone carving of a Roman blacksmith (300 B.C.)

ancient pliers

modern pliers

Files and Sandpaper

Files were first made in ancient Egypt. The interesting thing about making files is the teeth. The first teeth were made by hand with a hammer and a **chisel**. Later, machines were able to make the tiny teeth that let a file do its work.

The first sandpaper was made in China in the 1200s. Crushed seeds, sand, and shells were glued to **parchment**. Later, sharkskin was used. In modern times, glass was used. Today, many types of materials are used, but sand and paper usually are not!

This ancient file is made from hard stone.

Files are used to shape wood and other materials. As you can see, they haven't changed much!

Two different file textures, or tooth sizes, are shown.

There are more than 10,000 different types of files today!

Sandpaper comes in many different colors and textures. Some are rougher than others. Different textures are used to sand different materials.

The Finishing Touch

The years to come are sure to include tools that we cannot imagine today. But some tools will still look a lot like the ones ancient people used. Why change what works? As the saying goes, "If it isn't broken, don't fix it!"

Top Tools

A recent survey listed the 20 most important tools in history. How would you use these tools?

1	2	3	4	5	6	7	8	9
knife	abacus	compass	pencil	harness	scythe	rifle	sword	eyeglass

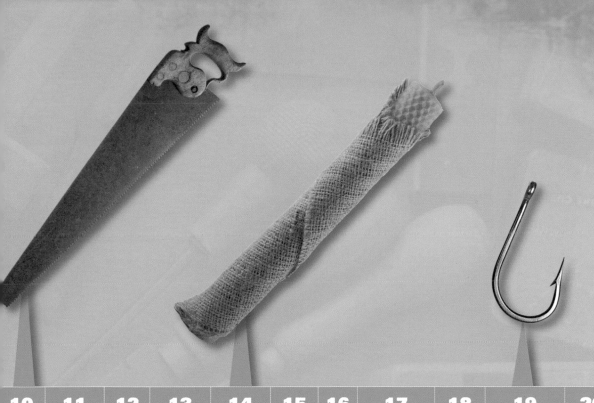

10	11	12	13	14	15	16	17	18	19	20
saw	watch	lathe	needle	candle	scale	pot	telescope	level	fishhook	chisel

Glossary

atoms—the smallest pieces of an element

chisel—a metal tool with a cutting edge at the end of a blade, used to shape or chip away at solid material

equipment—materials or supplies used in a specific activity

hardware store—a store where tools are sold

hatchets—small axes with a short handle

Industrial Revolution—the time when people started using machines and factories instead of tools to make things

materials—supplies used to do or make something

Middle Ages—the period of European history from about A.D. 500–A.D. 1500

molecules—the smallest pieces of a substance

opposable thumbs—thumbs that are capable of being placed against one or more of the remaining digits of a hand or a foot

parchment—the skin of a sheep or a goat prepared as writing material

sinew—a tough cord or band made from animal tendon

Stone Age—the oldest period in which human beings are known to have existed; noted for the use of stone tools

tongs—a device that usually consists of two moving pieces and is used to take hold of something

trades—business, work, or jobs

utensils—devices used in a household, especially in a kitchen

Index

animals, 4, 11, 13, 18, 22

arrow, 12, 15

axes, 22–23

bow 12, 15

bulldozer, 6

chimpanzee, 4, 8

China, 5, 26

chisel, 26, 29

chopsticks, 4–5

cranes, 6–7

equipment, 6–7

Egypt, 6, 26

Egyptians, 6, 9, 23

file, 26

Greeks, 23–24

hammer, 7, 9, 18, 24

hands, 10–11

hatchet, 14–15

Industrial Revolution, 18

kitchen tools, 20–21

materials, 6, 26–27

Middle Ages, 16, 21

opposable thumbs, 11

parchment, 26

pliers, 24–25

Romans, 21, 23–25

sandpaper, 26–27

saw, 22–23, 29

sewing tools, 20

spears, 15

Stone Age, 8

termites, 4

tongs, 5, 24–25

utensils, 5

water mills, 15

windmills, 15

woodworker, 16

About the Author

Dona Herweck Rice grew up in Anaheim, California, and graduated from the University of Southern California with a degree in English and from the University of California at Berkeley with a credential for teaching. She has been a teacher in preschool through tenth grade, a researcher, a librarian, and a theater director, and is now an editor, a poet, a writer of teacher materials, and a writer of books for children. She is married with two sons and lives in Southern California.